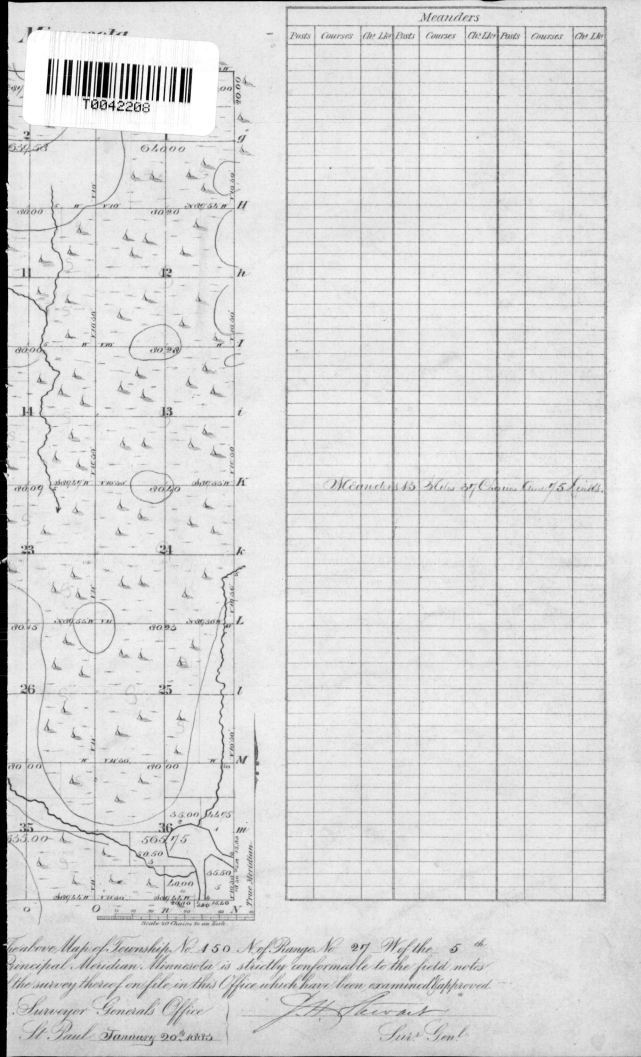

			Meanders					
Posts	Courses	Chs Lks	Posts	Courses	Chs Lks	Posts	Courses	Chs Lks

Meanders 13 Miles 37 Chains and 75 Links.

Scale 40 Chains to an Inch

The above Map of Township No. 150 N of Range No. 27 W of the 5th Principal Meridian Minnesota is strictly conformable to the field notes of the survey thereof on file in this Office which have been examined & approved.

Surveyor General's Office
St Paul January 20th 1883

J. H. Stewart
Survr Genl

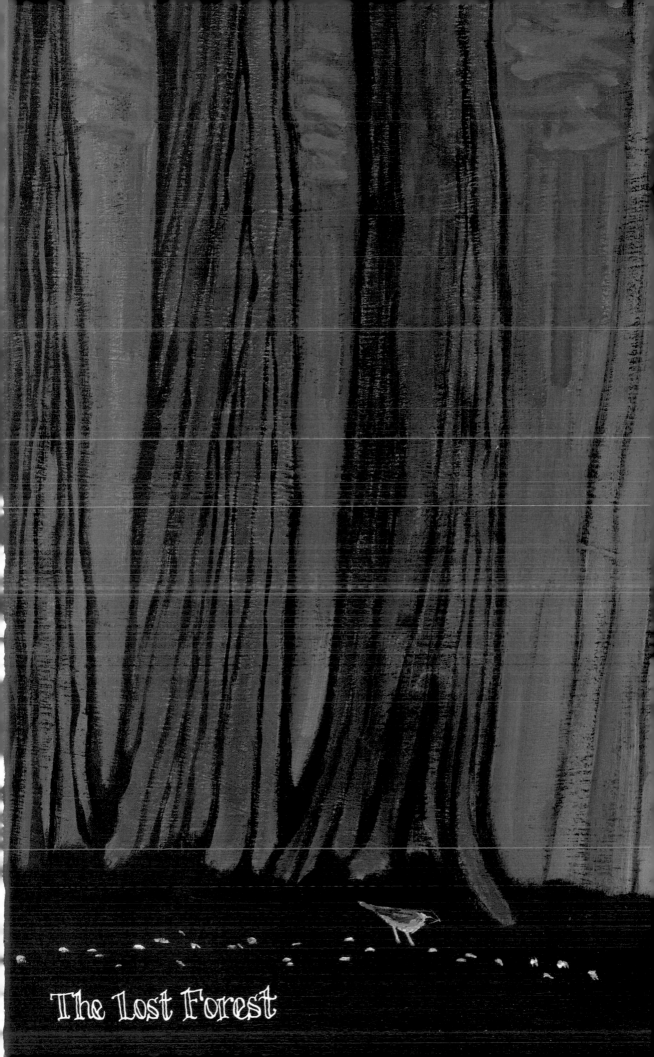

The Lost Forest

The Lost Forest

by Phyllis Root

illustrations by Betsy Bowen

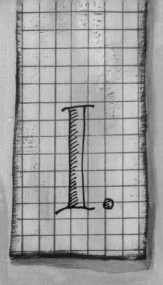

How do you lose a forest?

First you need a forest to lose.
A forest like the red pines and white pines
that once towered in Minnesota,
trees that had never been logged.

Trees so tall
you had to crane your head back
and even then you couldn't see their tops.
Trees so big
two people could hardly wrap their arms
around a single trunk.

|---4 ft. 6" diameter---→| Perimeter
of white pine =
14.156 ft.

Equivalent to =
2.57 Human
armspans

or

28 chickadees
beak to tail

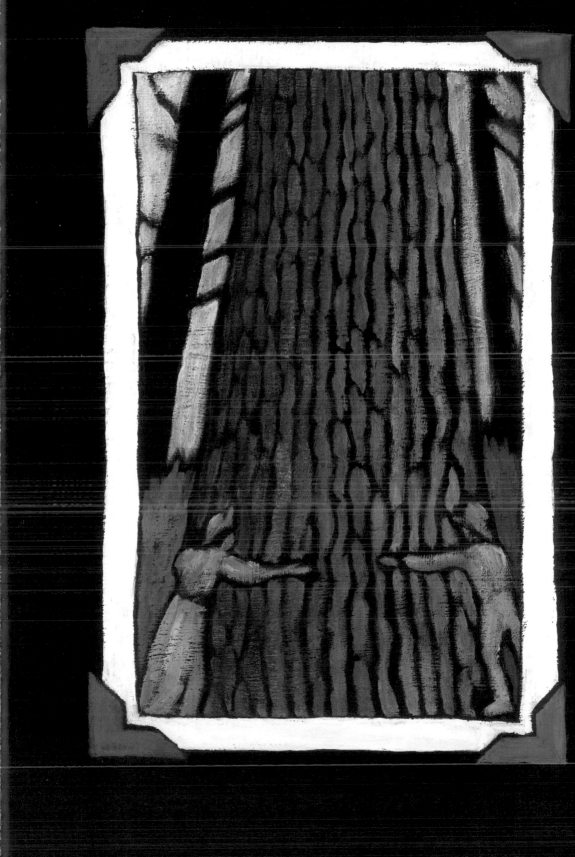

You might think a forest would be hard to lose.
But in Minnesota in 1882
a survey crew lost a forest.
Among those tall trees
black bears scratched for grubs,
moose drank at creeks,
eagles nested,
red-backed salamanders laid eggs in old logs,
and tiny coral-root orchids grew.

But the forest was lost, and it stayed lost,
while those tall trees kept growing taller.

Coral-root Orchids
8.5 inches

Land rolling
Heavily covere
balsa
Jac

Red-backed salamander
5.5 inches - eggs .35 inches

Bald
Eagles

63.5 ft.

dead
white
pine

d rate
marac with aspen
— and scattering
ine.
young Aspen & Birch
undergrowth

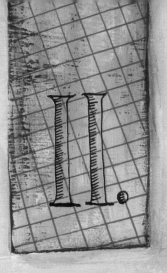

II.

The United States was growing, too.
In 1785 the Continental Congress
    passed a law
to survey all the land in the new nation.

Native people had lived and hunted,
    harvested and fished
on the land for thousands of years.
The land took care of them,
    and they took care of the land.
But the government of the United States
    wanted their land,
wanted that land to own and sell.
By the time the survey reached northern
    Minnesota,
most of the land had been taken from
    Native people,
and survey crews were sent to divide up
    that land.

Forests and prairies,
swamps, lakes, and ponds,
rivers and springs,
caves and quarries,
veins of ore and coal—
everything had to be measured
    and mapped
before it could be sold.

The surveyors used compasses to find their way.
They measured distances with poles and tally pins
and chains that were 66 feet long.
They carried axes to cut compass bearings on trees.
They took notebooks to write the measurements they made.

They mapped out townships
six miles wide and six miles long,
with borders running north to south and east to west,
a grid of land.

They divided the townships into sections.

They divided the sections into quarter sections.

And at every corner of every township
and every section
and every quarter section
the survey crew cut marks on trees
or planted posts with bearing marks
to locate each piece of land.

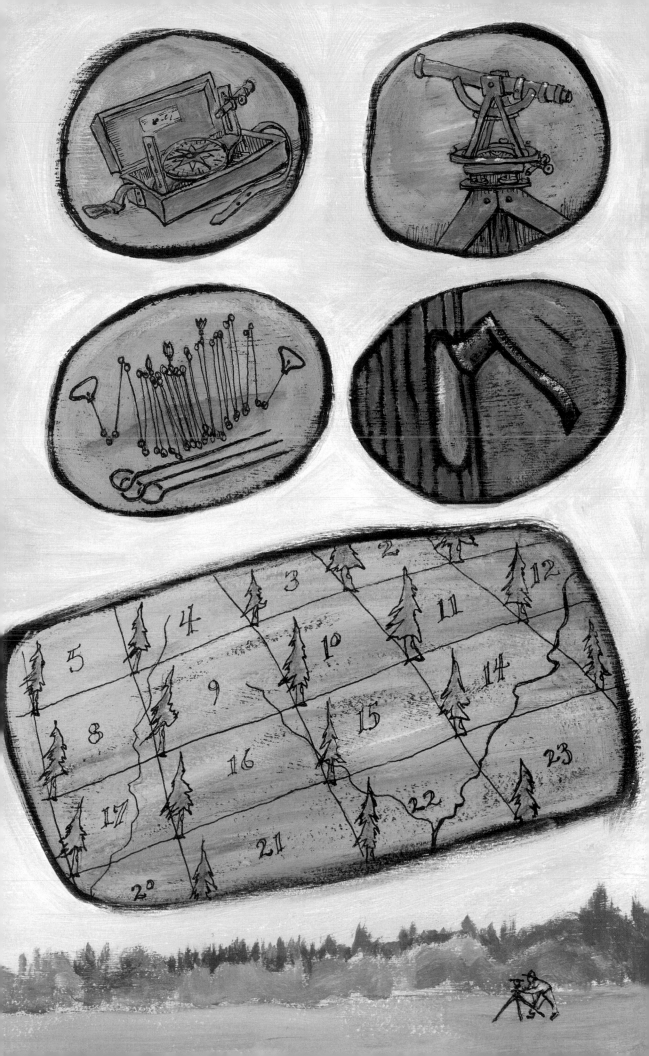

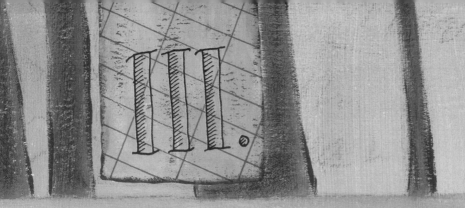

Year by year, surveyors measured their way
across territory that became the states
Ohio, Indiana, Illinois, Michigan, Wisconsin, Iowa,
Minnesota.

In the fall of 1882
Josiah R. King and his three-man crew were hired to survey
three townships in the state of Minnesota.

flour
pork
beans
dried apples
rice
coffee
matches

cornmeal
lard
salt
pepper
peas

The crew brought all the things they needed
to live on the land for months at a time:

> *a canvas tent to sleep in*
> *blankets to sleep under*
> *flour and pork and beans*
> *dried apples and rice and coffee*
> *matches and frying pans and pails*
> *a piece of cloth to use when mixing bread dough*
> *extra nails for mending boots.*

The surveyors wore wool hats,
coats with waterproof pockets,
roomy pants of sturdy fabric,
flannel underclothes and wide-soled boots,
and a large silk handkerchief
to keep mosquitoes, gnats, and moose flies
off their ears and necks.

  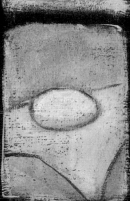 

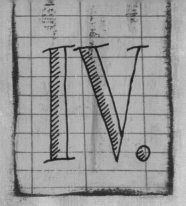

If you have ever walked through the woods
you know the land doesn't care
about straight lines.
Ridges rise up,
streams meander,
swamps sink underfoot.

If you were trying to turn this rollicking land
into straight lines on paper,
you might make a mistake.
Josiah King did.

On a blustery cold November day
he and his crew marked the corner of
Township 150
Range 27
Section 34
and drew the map for Coddington Lake
about half a mile farther north
than the lake actually was.

Maybe they were in a hurry to get home before winter.
Maybe they were confused
by the swampy land.
Whatever happened,
Josiah King wrote in his surveyor's notes:
"Water very clear and deep—abounding in fish—
There is no Pine Timber in the Township."

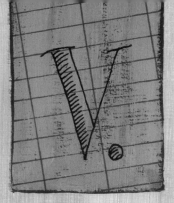

Anyone who wanted to buy land—
lumber barons, land companies, settlers—
looked at the maps that were drawn
from the survey crew's notes
and saw a lake instead of a forest.

All around those forgotten tall trees
(and all across most of Minnesota)
lumberjacks cut down the forests
with crosscut saws and axes,
dragged the tree trunks to rivers,
floated them downstream to be sawed into lumber
and made into houses and railroad ties
and oxcarts to carry settlers to Winnipeg.

All around Township 150
Range 27
Section 34
the forest disappeared,
trees and orchids,
animals who had lived among the trees,
birds who had nested in them—
gone.

But no lumber company wanted to buy land
that the map showed as a lake.
There was no profit in lake water,
so that forest stayed lost
and those tall trees kept growing.

For seventy-six years those "lost" trees
belonged to nobody but themselves,
just as they always had.
Skunks dug burrows.
Ovenbirds called *teecher teecher teecher*.
Woodpeckers hammered dead trees for insects.
Ruffed grouse drummed.
Foxes had pups who grew up to have pups
who grew up to have pups.
Moccasin-flowers and bunchberries bloomed in the spring.
Wind blew snow off pine boughs in winter.

Fire claimed some of the trees.
Wind felled others.
But most of those tall pines just grew taller and taller.

VII.

Then, in 1958, someone (probably a forest ranger)
noticed those tall trees,
and a crew came to measure and mark the land.

The surveyors discovered that
Township 150, Range 27, Section 34
wasn't a lake at all,
but a piece of land one mile square
covered with trees
that had never been cut,
growing on land that had never been sold.

Almost nowhere else in Minnesota had trees
like the trees of that lost forest
where the wind blew through the same branches
it had blown through three hundred years before.

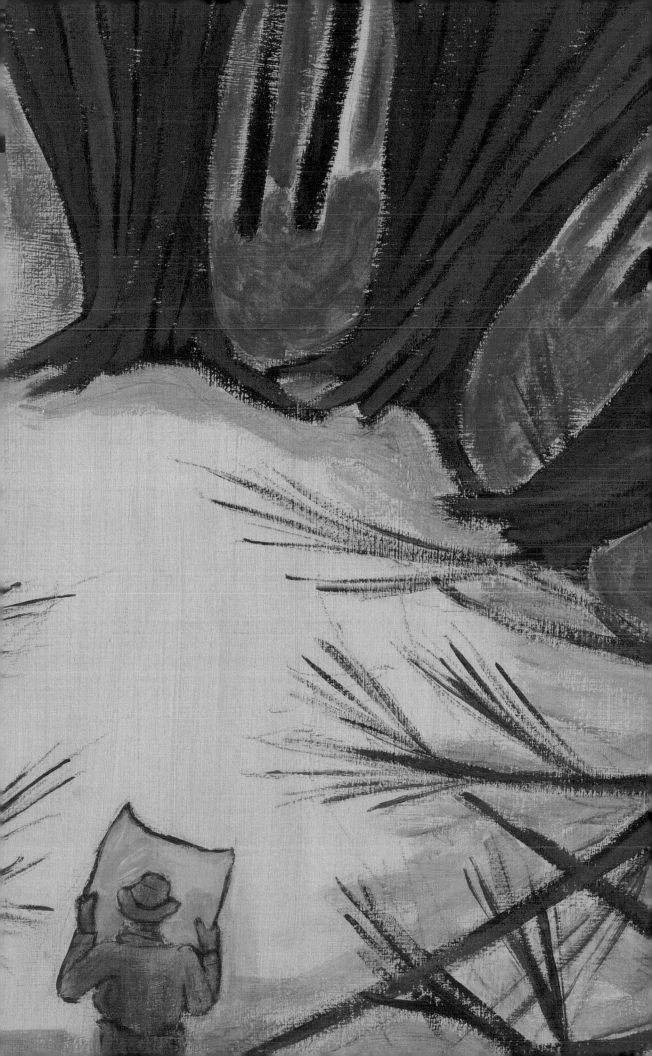

All the land around those tall trees
was National Forest now:
those tall trees were protected forever.

That forgotten part of the forest was 114 acres.
But because land was often sold in forty-acre parcels,
and because the forest had been lost and found again,
people called it the Lost Forty.

The trees had never really been lost.
Neither had the orchids, the moose, the warblers,
the weasels, the porcupines, the flycatchers, or the flickers.
They had always belonged to themselves.

But because Josiah King and his three-man survey
    crew made a mistake,
because they misplaced a lake on a map for
    seventy-six years,
you can go today and walk under trees so tall
you have to crane your neck to see their tops.
You can try to wrap your arms around a white pine tree
that is 350 years old.
You can walk through time and see the woods
as it used to be
and still is
in the Lost (and found) Forest.

WHAT IS AN OLD GROWTH FOREST?

Forest once covered about a third of Minnesota, but logging companies cut down almost all of those trees. Old growth forests (forests that have been growing for at least 120 years without any major disturbance) are rare.

How can you tell if you are walking among old growth trees? The trees will be different ages and heights, but most of them likely will be tall. Fire may have harmed some trees, but their thick bark and high branches help protect them. Wind may blow some trees over, and old age might fell others. Some dead trees, called snags, may still be standing, and others that have fallen lie on the ground decaying, their tipped-up roots leaving holes in the forest floor. Younger trees grow into the openings left by these fallen or burnt trees.

Old growth forests provide habitat for many plants and animals. Ospreys and bald eagles nest in old growth forest. Some songbirds, woodpeckers, hawks, and owls prefer old growth forest to forests that have been cleared and regrown. Fallen trees shelter small reptiles, mammals, and insects, and snags provide food and homes for many species of birds and mammals. Orchids (some tiny, some not so tiny) may grow among other native flowers on the forest floor. You might see more dragonflies, and more varieties of dragonfly, in lakes and streams near old growth forests.

WHO FOUND THE LOST FORTY?

Records don't indicate who exactly noticed the tall trees. We do know that the chief of the U.S. Forest Service wrote a letter dated December 2, 1958, in which he requested a resurvey of an area of more than one hundred acres that had been missurveyed "either through gross error or fraud." Even though the original survey showed a lake, the trees in the "lake" were more than two hundred years old.

Most likely, a forest ranger noticed the trees. Who actually "found" the lost forest is a mystery that someone might solve someday. Whoever it was helped to preserve a section of old growth forest, a glimpse of what much of northern Minnesota used to be, a walk back in time.

WHERE TO SEE OLD GROWTH FOREST IN MINNESOTA

Old growth forests are rare, and they are not all the same. A pine forest, a hardwood forest, or an oak forest are all different types of woodlands. Because lumber barons especially valued the tall white pines of northern forests, these old growth forests are especially rare today. In Minnesota, fewer than two thousand acres of old growth pines still stand. Where can you still walk through time among tall pine trees? Here are a few places:

- **The Lost Forty Scientific and Natural Area in Chippewa National Forest near Blackduck, Minnesota**

- **Itasca State Park near Park Rapids, Minnesota**

- **Minnesota Point Pine Forest Scientific and Natural Area in Duluth, Minnesota**

- **Eagle's Nest Island No. 4 Scientific and Natural Area near Bear Head Lake State Park near Ely, Minnesota**

- **Burntside Islands Scientific and Natural Area in Burntside Lake near Ely, Minnesota**

- **Purvis Lake–Ober Foundation Scientific and Natural Area near Ely, Minnesota**

- **Scenic State Park near Bigfork, Minnesota**

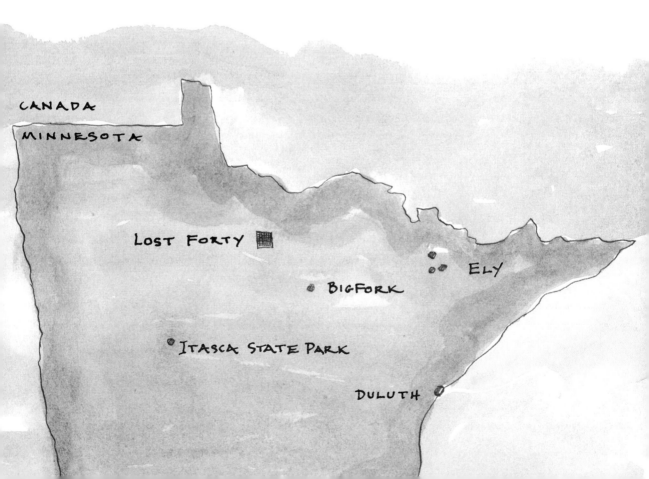

WHAT LIVES IN AN OLD GROWTH FOREST?

All of the plants and animals in this book may live in old growth pine forests. If you go to the Lost Forty (or another old growth forest), pretend you are a surveyor—but instead of looking for minerals, springs, and salt licks, look for these old growth inhabitants. Here are some of the species you might find.

1. Red pine *(Pinus resinosa)*
Red pine trees have reddish bark and needles that grow in bundles of two.

2. Eastern white pine *(Pinus strobus)*
Eastern white pine trees have soft needles in bundles of five. The bark is grayish brown.

3. Early coral-root *(Corallorhiza trifida)*
Early coral-root orchids might be hard to find because they are small and mainly colored green or yellow-green.

4. Spotted coral-root *(Corallorhiza maculata* var. *maculata)*
Spotted coral-root orchids have bright purple or red spots on their petals.

5. Moccasin-flower *(Cypripedium acaule)*
Moccasin-flower orchids (also called stemless lady's-slipper) have large pink pouches that bees must crawl through to gather pollen.

6. Hooker's orchid *(Platanthera hookeri)*
Hooker's orchids have yellow-green flowers with hook-shaped petals.

7. Bluebead lily *(Clintonia borealis)*
Bluebead lilies have yellow flowers in the spring that turn into small blue berries (which are *not* good to eat).

8. Bunchberry *(Cornus canadensis)*
The white petals on bunchberries develop into red berries that birds often eat.

9. Bald eagle *(Haliaeetus leucocephalus)*
Bald eagles need tall, strong trees for their nests, which might weigh more than a thousand pounds. Each year they add more to their nest.

10. Downy woodpecker *(Picoides pubescens)*
Minnesota's smallest woodpeckers have a white belly, a black and white back, and a small red spot on the back of the head.

11. Hairy woodpecker *(Picoides villosus)*
Hairy woodpeckers look very much like downy woodpeckers except they are larger and have longer beaks.

12. Ovenbird *(Seiurus aurocapilla)*
With olive backs and spotted breasts, ovenbirds blend into the forest floor. They cover their nests with leaves so that the nests look like tiny outdoor ovens.

13. Least flycatcher *(Empidonax minimus)*
These small brownish birds migrate north for the summer and need mature forest to nest.

14. Northern flicker *(Colaptes auratus)*
These large brownish woodpeckers have a yellow patch on the back of the neck and yellow linings in their wings, which are visible when they fly.

15. Ruffed grouse *(Bonasa umbellus)*
Ruffed grouse are about the size of chickens. They nest on the ground. You might hear males in the spring when they drum with their wings to attract mates.

MEASURING THE LAND

Land can be measured in different ways. One older method describes the land. Someone might sell a field marked by the large oak tree in one corner, a bend in the creek in another corner, and the pile of rocks in a third corner. These pieces of land might be any size or shape.

Dividing land into a grid of squares, however, made the land easier to sell. In 1785 Congress approved a cadastral survey; *cadastral* means finding and marking the boundaries of a piece of land. The government sent surveyors throughout the country.

A surveying team carried a **chain**, **tally pins**, and **compass**. The chain was exactly one hundred links long and measured 66 feet. The surveyors used a compass to determine a north–south or east–west line to follow. A chainman held one end of the chain while another chainman carried the other end along that line. If trees or brush grew in the way, an **axman** cut them down. When the chain was stretched in a straight level line, the chainman who had been moving the chain forward put a tally pin in the ground; the other chainman came to that tally pin, and the entire process was repeated. When they had measured

Surveyor's chain. 100 links, 66 feet long, markers every 10 links.

one mile, a post was put in the ground and **blazes** were cut in nearby trees. Each piece of land could be identified by its individual township number, range number, and section number, which were cut into a bearing tree.

A surveyor carried a **notebook**: he wrote down all these numbers and any information about the land being surveyed. **Plats** (maps that show property boundaries) were then drawn from these notes.

Sometimes surveying mistakes were made. Surveyors might be in a rush and make careless measurements. Instruments could break. A large deposit of iron ore could throw off a compass reading. A river or lake could interfere with those straight lines.

Today we have maps, aerial surveys, global positioning satellites, even pictures of the Earth from space. But in 1785 surveyors had none of these things. On foot, chain by chain, mile by mile, they inched their way across the United States.

If you look at a map or fly in a plane over the Midwest or the West, you can see the straight lines laid out by the surveyors in the borders of fields and farms and in the roads between them.

HOW TO TALK LIKE A SURVEYOR

Acre: a basic unit of measurement for the cadastral survey. An acre measured ten chains (660 feet) by one chain (66 feet).

Axman: the person on the survey team who chopped down trees and cleared away bushes in the way of the survey chain, as well as cutting the blazes on bearing trees.

Bearing tree: a tree marking a measured corner. Marks for township (T), range (R), and section (S) were cut into the trunk of the tree, and the tree's size and species were recorded in the surveyor's notebook.

Blaze: a mark on a bearing tree made by removing a little bark and carving the survey's location of the tree into the bare wood.

Cadastral: having to do with the boundaries of a piece of land.

Chain: Gunter's chain (invented by Edmund Gunter in 1620) was used in surveys for measuring. Each chain was exactly 100 links or 66 feet long.

Chainman: one of two people who carry the end of a chain on a surveying team.

Flagman: member of a survey team who marks a survey line for the chainmen to follow.

Meander line: a line indicating the curving banks of a lake or river.

Plat: a drawing or map made from a surveyor's notes to show what the surveyed land looked like.

Section: a square piece of land 80 chains (one mile) on each side, for a total of 640 acres.

Surveying: measuring and locating lines, angles, and elevations of land.

Tally pin: a pin used to keep track of how many chains had been measured; it was put into the ground plumb with the end of the chain. A pair of chainmen carried eleven tally pins.

Township: a square area of thirty-six sections, totaling six miles on each side.

HOW TO DRESS LIKE A SURVEYOR

Surveyors worked in all weather and all conditions. They might have to wade through swamps, sink into muck, or stare down a bear. Some surveyors even drowned. A manual for surveyors listed what they should wear to be ready for just about anything.

Here's how to dress like a nineteenth-century surveyor from the inside out:

- **Flannel underclothes all year round**
- **Trousers made of strong cloth, cut large**
- **A light coat with waterproof pockets to keep books and papers dry**
- **Boots with narrow fronts, wider backs, and thick soles with nails in them for good traction**
- **Wool hat**
- **A large silk neckerchief to keep bugs off**

The Eastern half of this Township is low and flat — soil 4th rate —
the Western portion is rolling and broken — 3rd rate soil — Timber
consists principally of Birch aspen spruce cedar & Tamarac — Scattering
clumps of Jack Pine in the Western portion of the Township — a dense
undergrowth of Young aspen & ash throughout the township —

The Lakes in the Township have high rolling banks — Water very
clear and deep — abounding in fish — There is no Pine Timber in the
Township — No springs — Mineral — or trails were observed. The creek
extending from N.W. to S.E. diagonally thro the Township is of a uniform
width navigable for Canoes its entire length — It passes thro Tamarac &
spruce swamps its entire length — The Bow String River passes in and out
of the Township in the South East corner of the town —

Best Pine in Northern Minnesota
Blackduck Area
Early 1900's

#20

TOWNSHIP 150 NORTH, RANGE 27 WEST, FIFTH PRINCIPAL MERIDIAN, MINNESOTA
SURVEY OF OMITTED LAND, SECTION 34

If you would like to see Josiah R. King's journals and maps from his notebooks, you can go to the Bureau of Land Management's website and find digitized versions. Go to www.glorecords.blm.gov, and choose **Survey** under **Search Documents**, then look for the Original Survey by Josias R. King in Itasca County, Minnesota.

Township № 150 N. Range № 27 W. 5ᵗʰ Me

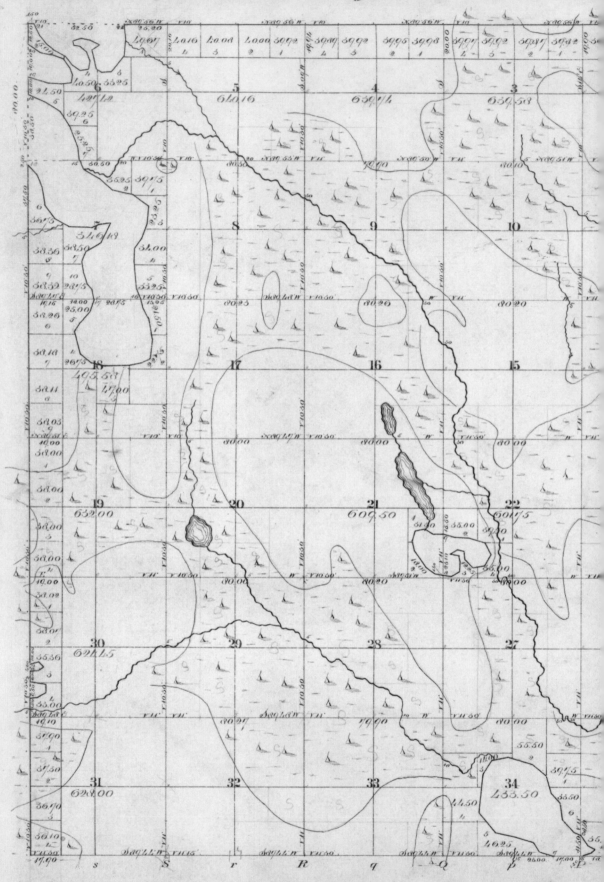

Area of Public Land 21998.19 Acres of Water Surface 993.47 Acres Total number of Acres 22991.66.

Surveys designated	By whom surveyed	Date of Contract	Amount of surveys M Chs Lks	When surveyed	Mean declination
Township lines N	J. P. Hinchilwood	June 7ᵗʰ 1875		1875	
S	J. R. King	Feby 10ᵗʰ 1882		1882	10° 45′ 00″
W & E	J. R. King	Feby 10ᵗʰ 1882	11. 79. 20	1882	
Subdivisions	J. R. King	Feby 10ᵗʰ 1882	59. 40. 40	Commenced Nov 10ᵗʰ 1882 Completed Dec 1ˢᵗ	
Meanders			15. 31. 15		